I am Barry MacDonald. I received the *dharma* name *Tekkan*, which means "Iron Man," a settled practitioner of great determination.

First Printing, 2022
ISBN 979-8-9867262-1-2

To contact Tekkan please email:
buddhaboy1289@gmail.com

This book is dedicated to my friends in the recovery from alcoholism community, without whom I couldn't be sane and sober.

The otter on the front cover, and the eagle on page iii were painted by the fabulous Will Ersland. The other drawings were done by my resplendent daughter, Jocelyn Figueroa.

Table of Contents

Everyday Mind XXIX

A Romp Through the Alphabet

O

Do you notice the perfection of the
letter "o" — of how the lips imitate
the shape of "o" — of how the tongue hollows
and resonates — the cheeks reverberate —
the breath effusively flows with its tone —
and of how "o" harmonizes with a
state of being — *of an adoration* —
of an unanticipated delight
spontaneously and totally felt?
but one letter does not a language make —
"o" is grafted onto other symbols
and attached to various meanings but
whenever it enunciates its full-
bodied resonance — *there is holiness* —

Opalescence
Apollo
totally
tomato
oval
flow
rose
toes
holy
bold
go
o.

У

When the superfluities are stripped and
we are left with the bare essence of life
the natural response for people is
the question “y” — and we begin asking
as little tykes as soon as we notice
a you and me and mine and yours without
in some cases ever getting a good
answer — and we don’t need to slather on
a “w” and “h” before the sound
and a frivolous curlicue after —
as the fact is we don’t know what we
desire to know which is such trouble so
we purse our lips together and then stretch
them enunciating a *whiny* noise.

y
but

n

"N" is a most ferocious negative
force of life denoting opposition
and frustration — which is ironic as
when we say "n" the tongue rises to the
roof of the mouth and vibrates which is a
lovely sound — but when we expostulate
"n" at the beginning of a word it
becomes aggressive as we fling the tongue
forward asserting a horrible clout
of nastiness — which could be compared to
the horde of Attila the Hun riding
from over the far horizon to lay
waste to sophisticated quietude —
as we never get all that we desire —

nattering nabobs of negativity
nugatory
nonsense
neither
never
nothing
nasty
nuts
not
nor
nag
no.

S

"S" symbolizes the dexterity
of the vibration of the tip of the
tongue — and the anonymous artist who
created the letter imitated
the utterance of the hissing and the
slithering sinuous motion of a
snake slinking over the ground — and you may
notice that the gap between a word that
ends with "s" and a word that starts with "s"
i*s sticky* — as is the case with these words —
euphoniou*s* *s*yllable*s* *s*ignify
the ceasele*ss* *s*ubtle sounds of the living
earth — what is more hypnotizing than a
sly glistening serpent that slink*s* *s*lips *s*lides?

There's a hint of a devil in the words
suspicious
slatternly
slippery
slimy
sleazy
sneaky
snooker
sticky
smooth
slam.

W

The sound of “w” is a stretching
of the lips combined with a throaty push
of breath that is a kind of a grunting
that doesn’t bloom into a querulous
and nagging and irrepressible “y” —
as by itself it is diminutive —
as if lacking independent substance —
even though it is called a double “u”
while it appears to be a double “v” —
which is a misnomer that somebody
should do something about — and look how it
is used with the words “hole” and “whole” which is
exactly the same sound attached to a
paradoxical mixture of meanings.

“w”
sometimes
blossoms
into
who
what
when
where
why
whatever.

d

The letter “d” is like the letters “b”
and “p” as it is a crisp bursting of
sound of a percussive quality much
like the beat of a drum — as “d’ is an
explosive thrusting forward of the tongue —
and often at the beginning of words
its meaning takes on a declarative
and decisive quality not at all
wishy-washy — denoting the facts that
are difficult if not impossible
to dismiss — which pushed to an extreme could
result in *damnation doggonit* — and
when designating the delicacies
in delicatessens it’s definitive.

“D” is given to clear-cut
definitions that sometimes
go to an extreme as in
determinism
destruction
depression
doomsday
d day
dark
drat
damn
dog.

C

"C" is a cipher as it manifests
either with the sound of a "k" that comes
from the fleshy rear of the roof of the
mouth — with a harsh cluck of breath — or with a
hiss of the vibrating tip of the tongue
like an "s" — which to me is evidence
that the committee of geniuses who
codified the alphabet were intent
on having 26 letters and they
added one near the start — or they became
enamored with the semicircular
symbol that they crafted and they *had to*
foist it into the collection somehow —
or they simply weren't paying attention.

The "c" may be viewed
as the outline of
a crescent moon which
is an emblem I
am enamored with.

V

"V" is a puff of air made with pursed lips —
the tip of the tongue is often paired with
qualities of luxury and prestige
reserved for the upper echelon of
societal accomplishment — with a
little irony here and there — as with
vasectomy and valium — which are
civilized vices — and observe the dash
and precision and simplicity of
the design of "v" as it bespeaks a clean
bold and decisive character that would
never comport with the *déclassé* the
caboodle the *clumsy* the *squalid*
and the *slipshod mess* of humanity —

valedictorian
virtuosity
voluptuous
vivacious
victory
verity
virtue
valid
velvet
Vince.

m

The initial enunciation of
"m" is done with the lips closed — and the tongue
is subordinate — and the lips hum with
vibration as they open with a breath —
and as words are like transient birds
"hummingbird" is a good example of
the resonation reverberating
off of the teeth with a yummy playful
quality — while the meanings coupled with
"m" include a menagerie as with
majestic monuments or minuets
performed by maestros or a motley horde
of mongrels and mangled monsters
mesmerizing in their maladjustment —

magnificent
miserable
monkey business
mordant
money
morsel
minute *(as in time)*
minute *(as in small)*
magnet
mouse
must
mutt.

u

I admire the symbol of the letter
"u" as it looks like a womb that is full
of a brilliant baby — while its sound is
made with a level vibrating tongue and
with oval lips that denote emotion —
which is a kissing cousin of a full-
bodied "o" when a person's happy and
contented — as if enjoying a cool breeze
on a hot day or tasting a pumpkin
pie — we might say that "u" possesses a
secret and sacred quality as it
may be used as a movement away
from the hungry grasping ego toward
an ennobling and majestic "*You.*"

"U" is elongated
with other letters
as in:
eau
oo
eu
ew.

f

"F" is a friction of air that comes when
the lips are pinched together and breath is
expelled in a burst as if a person
were about to whistle but suddenly
chickened out — and the capital "F" has
a formal appearance while the lower
case has a curlicue that looks like a
flick of hair — *with stubby arms across its*
middle — to me "f" serves as a brief spurt
of fricative modulation of mood
fascinatingly fantastically
versatile which can be frozen frantic
fractured frustrated focused and fubar —
amd one has to make an amusing face.

The letters "p-h" often
replicate its sound — as in
phantasmagoria.

t

If you were an ordinarily bored
child you would have discovered how to make
a snapping noise with the tips of your thumb
and middle finger which is the same kind
of sound as "t" when the upper tongue is
pressed against the roof of the mouth and then
"snapped" forward with a staccato effect —
which is a spice for a language that needs
some jazz to keep everyone awake — so
when you find yourself drifting off in the
afternoon you could tap your fingers on
a desk or toss troublesome words about
and pitch a tantrum tantamount to a
tricky toddler's grasping for *attention*.

Putting an "h" or
an "i-o-n" behind
a "t" is a guaranteed
buzzkill.

Z

A person's tongue is as skillful as a
ballerina twirling circles upon
the balancing of a toe — as is proved
by the virtuosity of the tip
of the tongue when performing either a
"s" or a "z" — while the difference is
a variation of vibration as
"z" throbs intensely — *in honor of the*
noble bumblebee — and gives to words a
vigorous energy — as with zip zap
and zigzag — imparting the zeal of a
zealot — and it's zippy in foreign tongues
as it's the *Zen* of *Zazen* in *Zendos*
and in Babylonian *ziggurats.*

The tongue partners
with the ears and
the filtering
mind.

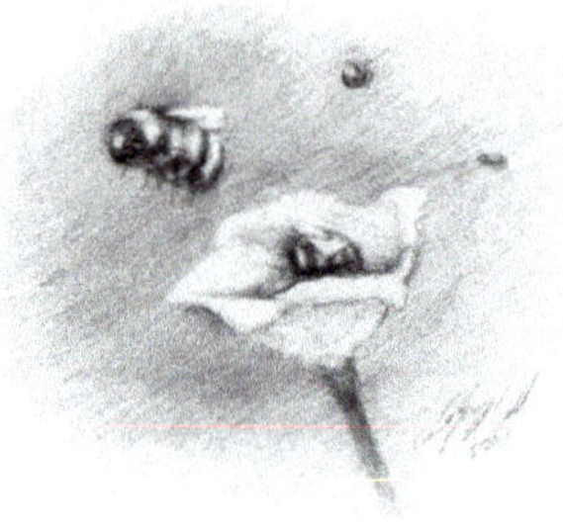

a

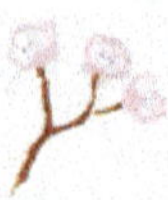

Being a poet who likes to rhyme and
who enjoys disguising my rhymes at the
end of lines I have discovered that one
neutered pronunciation of “a” rhymes
with “the” and its meaning gives *a* vague
recognition — for example that Bush
was *a* Republican but was also *the*
President — which is a *special* kind of
official — “t-h-e” has panache but
the single letter “a” does not — on the
other hand the clear and noble sound of
“a” arches the tongue near the roof of the
mouth and vibrates and there are hundreds of
words of any length that will rhyme with “a” —

flay
slay
betray
cliché
disobey
déclassé
auto-da-fe
radioactive decay.

e

Letter “e” is similar to “a” as
they both have cheerful shapes and are also
vowels which means that their sounds are crystal clear
without a flexing of the lips or tongue —
which makes them easy partners with other
sounds — and the position of the tongue when
saying “e” resembles “a” except that
e’s tone is higher — for habitual
wordsmiths there is no easier sound to
chime with at the beginning middle or
end of words as English is teeming with
“e” — and even slight enunciations
of “e” imitate happy golden bees
bouncing on a sunny glorious day —

flea
pea
easy
beauty
knock-knee
apogee
chickadee
Aegean Sea
petite bourgeoisie.

b

"B" is a boisterous burst of air that's
done with the flexing of the lips and not
the tongue — which makes a "bop" and not a "drop" —
as the lips are just as capable as
the tongue of percussion — I think of a
ball bouncing down a mountain stream bumping
off of rocks and boulders — and also of
the beautiful blue of the sky that is
bountiful with sunshine — *so much so as*
to bring me to believe the letter "b"
is blue — to be alive to be bemused
befuddled bewitched and bewildered is
part of our being — *to breathe a billion*
breaths — *to bloom a billion bedazzled thoughts.*

Using normal
conventions of
long and short vowels
shouldn't we be saying
Holy *Bib*-le?

p

The pop within a plop of a drop of
rain that plinks upon a pond or a pool
of rippling water is a version of
the jubilation imbued inside of
the percussive quality of the lips —
and oh how ponderous and propitious
is the joy of paying attention to
the puny details of the pitter and
patter of the expression of language —
as look how funny the letters “b” and
“p” become — *as both are pasted to an*
“o” which is a symbol for the holy —
while a “b” has a cat’s tail ascending —
a “p” has a doggie’s tail descending.

The art of
fashioning
a letter to
match the
quality of
sound is
exquisite.

r

A vibrating "rrr" is similar to
"sss" and "zzz" as they each embody the
resonation of the tongue — except that
the letters "s" and "z" evoke the sound
of the tip of the tongue — whereas letter
"r" represents the reverberation
of the entirety of a curled tongue —
approximate to the "grrr" of a dog
a bear or a tiger with a rough and
rugged aspect — and it's appropriate
that the symbol "s" was applied to a
swiveling snake — but it's a shame that a
design wasn't *embellished* to *relish*
the rasping of a ruthless rattlesnake.

Romeo's
romance
with
Juliet
was
reckless.

q

The pitch of "q" comes with a push of air
from the throat — the tongue at the back of the
mouth rises and falls with the thrusting of sound —
as "q" is one of several throaty and
breathy coos interwoven in English —
as a language arouses an array
of talents that escape the notice of
consciousness — and we bring this letter to
life by saying "q" with the vowel
"u" — but on its own it's not dramatic
but quiet and quick playing a role by
adding a quantum of energy to
our speech — who could quibble with querulous
questions about the quality of a cluck?

Letter "q" is like a dog
with a tail on the right —
with "p" the tail is on
the left.

k

The pronunciation of the letter
"k" is done with the clear resonation
of the vowel "a" — which enhances it with
a clarity which in daily usage
it lacks — as "k" is just a bit stronger
than the cluck of "q" — and when one recalls
that "c" also borrows the sound of "k"
in half of *c*'s enunciations one
wonders if we need such a subtle
slicing of utterance — perhaps after
all — *like everything else done by people* —
there's a haphazard mishmash at the core —
if only our inventors had been a
bit better *our language would be music.*

I am calm and cool
not querulous nor
cantankerous
keeping a keen
control of my
quizzical
quibbles.

g

There is a grunt of a breath ingrained in
the gritty expression of a “g” that
is similar to “q” and “k” — except
that there’s guttural force in the downward
thrust of the tongue at the back of the mouth —
and the import of the meaning of
its pitch gives an element of grandeur
to words with the letter “g” — as with good
and great and grand piano — and even
when the words aren’t glorious they do have
an impact — as “g” is distinctive and
difficult to ignore — as is shown with
grip and gripe and gallows and goblet and
grumble and granular grotesqueries.

I am grateful
for words like
gimp
gloom
goat
glint
glop
goof
guilt
gun
gimmick
glutton
gimlet eye.

j

"J" is a softening of "g" and on
occasion when "g" is followed by
"i" or "y" the "g" takes the sound of "j" —
as with *gypsy* and *gibberish* — "j" is
performed with a flexing of the middle
of the tongue — I was entranced with a word
when I was inexperienced in the
ways of love reading Shakespeare's "Romeo
and Juliet" — as Romeo watches
the sunrise on the morning after their
wedding night and he says to Juliet
" . . . *jocund* day stands tip toe on the misty
mountain tops" — and ever since this reading
of *"jocund" the letter "j" was joyous.*

There is joy
in the words
jamboree
jubilee
Jennifer
Juliet
Julia
Julie
July
jingle
jewel
jelly
jam.

h

If its neck were just a wee bit taller
the "h" would be a groovy symbol for
a giraffe — the sound of "h" is a push
of air formed by the pipe of the throat —
unlike many sounds of the alphabet the
tongue and lips do not resonate or flex
when the lungs express an "h" — so the "h"
is a clue to how much our breathing has
to do with our enunciating — there
isn't that much drama connected with
the letter — and you may notice many
quiet appearances of "h" within
these lines — but try saying words without the
help of inhaling and exhaling breath.

"H" is a helper that
doesn't take the limelight —
hot
hop
happy
harem
hoosegow
hard-headed
haphazard
happenstance.

1

The tip of the tongue resonates as it's
pressed against the roof of the mouth to make
the sound of "l" — and the pitch of "l" comes
from the flicking forward of the tongue — as
the ballet of language is breath inside
of motion with the aid of all parts of
the tongue the teeth the mouth and the throat — as
"l" is liquidly lackadaisical
lazy languorous lustrous and lonely —
even loony — and you may glance at these
lines of words and see how the letter "l"
is inlaid repeatedly in lower
case looking like the telephone poles on
our streets that don't catch and hold attention.

The formality of
capital "L" has a
rigid and strict look that
imposes dignity.

X

The "X" has the honor of having the
fewest words in the dictionary — when
not pronounced as an "x" it takes the sound
of "z" which makes one speculate why it
exists — as much like the letter "c" it's
a cipher — and yet the symbol of two
lines crossed in the middle has the charm of
primordial simplicity — easy
for innocents to write as signatures —
and on a map of desperadoes an
"x" was a cynosure for Blackbeard's gold
worthy of blunderbuss homicide —
wouldn't science fiction be diminished
without the sparkle of sexy x-rays?

When was the last
time you said
xyst
Xerox
Xerxes
xylophone?

i

The capital letter "I" could be viewed
as a prestigious Corinthian
column — the little "i" could be thought of
as the upright posture of a person
with a dot hovering above as an
emblem for an *eye* — as a token of
our human ability to see and
perceive — the "j" also has a floating
eye but with a monkey's tail that somewhat
lessens its dignity — the pristine sound
of "i" results from the vibrating dip
of the middle of the tongue that marries
a clear resonation with ideas
of piercing discerning intelligence.

In the impish
pronunciation
of "i" there is
irony —
illness
ignorance
imbecility
impurity
impetuousness.

Bicycle Sestina

I am happy and I am curious
the play of the seasons entrances me
a music of crickets is in the air
which is a sign of summer's ending
may I adore the crickets with my words?
the crickets thrill the cornfields afternoon

I see from a bicycle afternoon
the patterns of the summer are curious
may I net ephemera with my words?
as a panoply of detail escapes me
the sun is golden near summer's ending
the fleeting of daylight is in the air

swallows are swiftly turning in the air
swallows hunt by the river afternoon
their stay in Minnesota is ending
the pull of migration is curious
their marvelous movement entrances me
may I encumber swallows with my words?

may I distill the sunlight with my words?
a conclusion is approaching in the air
the quality of the *light delights* me
the sun is hotly shining afternoon
and yet the mellow twilights are curious
the *haze* and *blaze* of summer are ending

(*. . . continued from page 53*)

the burgeoning summer growth is ending
may I paint its fulfillment with my words?
a touch of weariness is curious
there are hints of a *pivot* in the air
shadow is evanescent afternoon
yet the decades of my life have schooled me

the stubbornness of the wind informs me
the bicycle season will be ending
I cherish a golden sparkle afternoon
may I celebrate moments with my words?
a tide of the season is in the air
diminishing sunshine is curious

the dance of sun and earth is curious
its momentum is passing in the air
may I capture its magic with my words?

The Verge of Autumn Villanelle

The sky is beautiful in September
the days are warm and lazy afternoon
the night extends its wings in November

the light becomes a glorious azure
in the morning there is a crescent moon
the sky is beautiful in September

the air is crisply transparent outdoors
the foliage will be coloring soon
the night extends its wings in November

the windows are cool when open indoors
the sun is a golden sparkle at noon
the sky is beautiful in September

temperate days are keen in October
with the flaming leaves and a silver moon
the night extends its wings in November

in October colder days are somber
a turning comes with the harvest moon
the sky is beautiful in September
the night extends its wings in November.

Politics is ugly by September
the accusations fly from Labor Day
airwaves are nasty until November

the ploy is to pique and marshal despair
channeling outrage is a power play
politics is ugly by September

30-second ads are caricatures
the twisting of facts are tricks of the trade
airwaves are nasty until November

repetitive slogans are doctrinaire
aggressive righteousness is on display
politics is ugly by September

perpetrators and victims are compared
an appeal for comeuppance is conveyed
airwaves are nasty until November

our bigotries and grievances are paired
could there possibly be a better way?
politics is ugly by September
airwaves are nasty until November.

Oh to be ensconced in a *La-Z-boy*
not needing to do a lick of labor
being recumbent is the way of joy

watching the T.V. is an easy ploy
with glitzy celebrities to savor
oh to be ensconced in a *La-Z-boy*

not having to trudge like the hoi polloi
the afternoon has a carefree flavor
being recumbent is the way of joy

seeing a movie of Helen of Troy
Poor Odysseus was such a *nutter*
oh to be ensconced in a *La-Z-boy*

with so much frivolity to enjoy
taking the time for a morning slumber
being recumbent is the way of joy

a cushy posture is the real McCoy
raising the feet in a blissful manner
oh to be ensconced in a *La-Z-boy*
being recumbent is the way of joy.

So much of *memory* is *peppery*
why did things happen the way that they did?
who's responsible for my memory?

what I remember is a travesty
I'd like an exuberant past instead
so much of *memory* is *peppery*

memory should be *complementary*
all of my grievances are better dead
who's responsible for my memory?

we each have dollops of rascality
I'd rather not be remorseful in bed
so much of *memory* is *peppery*

why can't I have a joyful panoply?
I recall so well the words that I said
who's responsible for my memory?

someone should emphasize my gallantry
a Grecian tragedy is in my head
so much of *memory* is *peppery*
who's responsible for my memory?

It's odd that I remember as I do
I'd like to be a *better forgetter*
who wants to be awake in bed and stew?

my nagging thoughts are a curious brew
how am I choosing what to remember?
it's odd that I remember as I do

my disturbing memories stick like glue
my mind's not doing me any favors
who wants to be awake in bed and stew?

I seem to be hunting for hidden clues
justifications have sour flavors
it's odd that I remember as I do

and also my fears assemble and queue
my head engages in useless labor
who wants to be awake in bed and stew?

I dwell very much on *what I am due*
I'm well aware my thoughts are palaver
it's odd that I remember as I do
who wants to be awake in bed and stew

My Kitcat is the simplest creature
he flops on the floor and shows his belly
his is a goofy curious nature

morning scrambles are a daily feature
he is entranced by treats that are smelly
my Kitcat is the simplest creature

when he is hungry he is a whiner
when he's *feisty* he is *Mr. Bitey*
his is a goofy curious nature

he jumps upon the refrigerator
and fancies himself a celebrity
my Kitcat is the simplest creature

he then becomes an instigator
he topples containers frivolously
his is a goofy curious nature

he is not ambitious and is not sour
and he doesn't need an identity
my Kitcat is the simplest creature
his is a goofy curious nature.

Soon I am going to be a grandfather
welcoming life under the *sun* and *moon*
as a newborn will *see* and *touch* and *breathe*
to be a member of society
having a loving mother and father
coming either as a daughter or son

taking a role as a daughter or son
later a grandmother or grandfather
having a turn as mother or father
exploring along with the *sun* and *moon*
navigating in our society
needing to learn to *see* and *touch* and *breathe*

it is magic to *see* and *touch* and *breathe*
happy either as a daughter or son
set within evolving society
inspiring to no end this grandfather
who's already lived with the *sun* and *moon*
who's paid his dues as a loving father

it may be hard on mothers and fathers
it's difficult to *see* and *touch* and *breathe*
there is hardship under the *sun* and *moon*
with burdens for either daughters or sons
memory is long for this grandfather
I have suffered fractured society

(. . . *continued from page 61*)

I have borne whiplashing society
difficulties test mothers and fathers
enough to encumber this grandfather
who is grateful to *see* and *touch* and *breathe*
we want the best for our daughters or sons
we take our chances with the *sun* and *moon*

our years are measured with the *sun* and *moon*
we forget our *vanished* society
life's precarious for daughters and sons
so much depends on mothers and fathers
we are lucky to *see* and *touch* and *breathe*
I cannot remember my grandfather

I met him only once — *my grandfather* —
within his days to *see* and *touch* and *breathe* —
one never ceases to be a father.

To be a pilot is to touch the sky
to have a talent that's beyond compare
what a gift it is to gracefully fly

how strange for a human to be so high
to *shake* with the turbulence in midair
to be a pilot is to touch the sky

to *see* from above the clouds — *and to spy* —
to be in control in the *air* is *rare*
what a gift it is to gracefully fly

with the bonds of gravity to defy
upward through a layer of clouds to tear
to be a pilot is to touch the sky

to observe the rivers and fields slip by
to comprehend the dangers and to dare
what a gift it is to gracefully fly

to see the earth with a majestic eye
to be *vibrantly alive* in the air
to be a pilot is to touch the sky
what a gift it is to gracefully fly.

The one splendid jewel is everywhere
from here it extends in each direction
it is the clarity that we could share

there's great simplicity in breathing air
we tangle circumstance with selection
the one splendid jewel is everywhere

a quiet interlude's beyond compare
we taint experience with rejection
it is the clarity that we could share

attending to clouds is not an error
we dazzle our heads with intellection
the one splendid jewel is everywhere

we could open our thoughts amid our cares
we lose our balance with introspection
it is the clarity that we could share

the poise of an empty moment is bare
relaxation helps with circumspection
the one splendid jewel is everywhere
it is the clarity that we could share.

We are honest in expressing our cares
they give me the gift of sincerity
then I'm able to see around corners

I have come to trust the words of my peers
they help me lose my insularity
we are honest in expressing our cares

each of us passes through dividing doors
I rely on our similarity
then I'm able to see around corners

all of us suffer from various fears
we each experience differently
we are honest in expressing our cares

a drunk will give of himself when he shares
this is the heartbeat of recovery
then I'm able to see around corners

we all have suffered from the tips of spears
in our stories we find a harmony
we are honest in expressing our cares
then I'm able to see around corners.

Each of us hears without interrupting
it's not helpful to be giving advice
we give to each other by listening

the pain of resentment is confusing
indulging bitterness comes with a price
each of us hears without interrupting

the denial of wrongs needs releasing
our belligerent natures are not nice
we give to each other by listening

the surrender of anger is freeing
imparting honesty is a device
each of us hears without interrupting

we hear some nonsense without commenting
booze is a parody of paradise
we give to each other by listening

we strengthen our efforts by relaxing
a reluctant beginning will suffice
each of us hears without interrupting
we give to each other by listening.

What is as slippery as an otter?
an otter's a curious animal
it's a whirling dervish in the water

it is slickly fleeting underwater
appropriate for fish — not a mammal —
what is as slippery as an otter?

it is *quick and nimble — not a plodder —*
an otter's playfulness is tangible
it's a whirling dervish in the water

an otter is a rascally swimmer
with an appetite that's insatiable
what is as slippery as an otter?

what is as versatile as an otter?
with land and water it's adaptable
it's a whirling dervish in the water

it's a dancer within a frigid river
its clever expression is affable
what is as slippery as an otter?
it's a whirling dervish in the water.

What is as majestic as an eagle?
as it lazily lingers in the sky
an eagle's fierce — it isn't affable —

its crushing talons are implacable
it hunts its prey with a discerning eye
what is as majestic as an eagle?

its finesse of wind is impeccable
from astonishing height it is a spy
an eagle's fierce — it isn't affable —

its grim spirit is unapproachable
its predation from a distance is sly
what is as majestic as an eagle?

for a fish it's incomprehensible
a sudden unexpected way to die
an eagle's fierce — it isn't affable —

its decisive striking is terrible
an eagle's bearing can't be prettified
what is as majestic as an eagle?
an eagle's fierce — it isn't affable.

What can we do when they're deceitful?
because I'm watching I know they're lying
I also see that they're not remorseful

their strategy's intricate and forceful
they don't answer questions — *which is telling* —
what can we do when they are deceitful?

public opinion's much too gullible
so much naiveté's disheartening
I also see that they're not remorseful

politicians are slickly flexible
they skew the meanings of words they're using
what can we do when they are deceitful?

it's sad to know propaganda's fruitful
the distortion of facts is frightening
I also see that they're not remorseful

I'd love to see them held accountable
hearing willful lies is dispiriting
What can we do when they are deceitful?
I also see that they're not remorseful.

Politicians tout heartfelt agendas
but be wary — *they don't do as they say* —
concocting a narrative is their biz

appeals for justice engender a buzz
we would all like to see the bigots pay
politicians tout heartfelt agendas

doomsday scenarios propagate fizz
the facts will be known by some future day
concocting a narrative is their biz

their ceaseless accusations are a whizz
inspiring a rage is easy play
politicians tout heartfelt agendas

it's difficult to spot the truth because
we forget the details of yesterday
concocting a narrative is their biz

who cares what a disgusting liar says
when a righteous fury is on display?
politicians tout heartfelt agendas
concocting a narrative is their biz.

The earth rotates a thousand miles an hour
we're sick of political narratives
the tides of seasons shift within the sky
human hearts hunger for sincerity
we watch the earth move at the horizon
can we be helpful with generous words?

can we make a difference with our words?
there's a babble of chatter every hour
competition colors our horizons
we each compose our private narratives
secrets are woven with sincerity
are we solicitous under the sky?

do we taste solitude under the sky?
are we hypnotized by unspoken words?
do we bear compromised sincerity?
how much can we transform within an hour?
do we endure punishing narratives?
do we fashion ominous horizons?

it is easy to forget horizons
to be unmindful of a cloudy sky
to be lost inside lazy narratives
to find comfort with conventional words
to dissipate our strain with mundane hours
to please ourselves with sour sincerity

(. . . continued from page 71)

does the earth engender sincerity?
does the earth impose frightful horizons?
does the planet divide itself with hours?
is it mindful of its breathable sky?
is it receptive to our human words?
does the earth have use for a narrative?

we compose the cosmos with narratives
it's hard to live without sincerity
we define ourselves with pivotal words
we are bound within a swift horizon
we scrutinize the stars beyond the sky
we measure our tribulations with hours

do we escape the constriction of hours?
does our consciousness resemble the sky?
do we live with unceasing horizons?

The grassroots groups have honest intentions
their messages bespeak sincerity
politics isn't their occupation

they scrounge for funds for their operations
they cannot doubt their moral clarity
the grassroots groups have honest intentions

they don't have corrupting obligations
they face nastiness with temerity
politics isn't their occupation

they've learned the details of legislation
their motivation comes from charity
the grassroots groups have honest intentions

they lack the money for litigation
they aim for a decent prosperity
politics isn't their occupation

they are worthy of our admiration
as bulwarks opposing barbarity
the grassroots groups have honest intentions
politics isn't their occupation.

September 11

Thousands suffered on that terrible day
like those within the collapsing towers
horror surpasses what words can convey

millions recoil from memory today
when terrorists achieved defining hours
thousands suffered on that terrible day

thousands of families were scarred that day
America witnessed the falling towers
horror surpasses what words can convey

heroics that day continue to play
courage imparts unsuspected power
thousands suffered on that terrible day

a nation *pivots* from its darkest days
we cannot forget our vanished towers
horror surpasses what words can convey

ordinary people deserved our praise
they withstood the fire — they didn't cower
thousands suffered on that terrible day
horror surpasses what words can convey.

There are documentaries of the day
people see the unimaginable
we can listen to what the voices say

cascading events repeatedly play
the impact of the planes is horrible
there are documentaries of the day

people are jumping from towers today
desperation is unforgettable
we can listen to what the voices say

there is courage and calm amid dismay
the falling towers are unstoppable
there are documentaries of the day

the courage of firemen is on display
their awful fate is irreversible
we can listen to what the voices say

the fight for survival's alive today
the trauma of terror is palpable
there are documentaries of the day
we can listen to what the voices say.

Pivoting Terza Rima

I can be unforgiving of myself
indulging bitter and punishing thoughts
disparaging and belittling myself

not noticing my thoughts are tied in knots
unable to grant myself clemency —
am I really that bad? — *no I am not*

I recognize my own severity
while practicing the art of relaxing
not trying to halt my ferocity

not suppressing but instead allowing
my thoughts to be *exactly what they are*
as I know they will be *dissipating*

it's a laugh to see that my mind's bizarre
and releasing nonsense has helped so far.

Underneath the madness there is a peace
I see that my head is a chatterbox
if I resist the noise it doesn't cease

indulging anger is Pandora's Box
I see the bitterness as what it is
letting it go involves a paradox

now it's not as difficult as it was
I aim to be as light as a feather
force doesn't do what relaxation does

behaving better makes it easier
a pivot toward gratitude does a trick
when I'm grateful my head is quieter

my first inclination's to be a prick
it helps immensely not to be so quick.

The watermelon season is ending
they won't be here at Aldi's anymore
the cycles of the earth are unbending

I have cycles at the grocery store
once in a week I circulate a cart
throughout the year blueberries are in store

it's time for the pumpkin season to start
it's easy to take these gifts for granted
I have such a lazy satisfied heart

the lives we are living are enchanted
so far we've been protected from trouble
we reap the fruit of what others planted

patterns of a life consist of struggle
as secure and stable as a bubble.

The politics of energy's in play
the farmers rely on fuel to be fruitful
without gas or diesel there is no way

for them to be prudently successful
opinions differ on ecology
on what is humanely beneficial

pundits tinker with the economy
demagogues demonize fuels and people
they dazzle people with doomsday theories

society's fabric isn't stable
prosperous societies are quite rare
as long as we're free we are capable

of nourishing ourselves with food to spare
as long as we slip the doomsayer's snares.

Show me how that these people aren't rotten
my opinions are often based on me
on ego striving — *and misbegotten* —

their power lusting is easy to see
and my livelihood is clearly threatened
it's true they are behaving wickedly

it's entirely rational to be scared
I'd like a reliable source of strength
and to sidestep the warping of hatred

I am seeking a reassuring warmth
an inner peace within activity
a compass that heartens me for the length

of the struggle — *something stronger than me* —
so I can wrangle *optimistically*.

Doors Sestina

We define ourselves with our boundaries
we fashion armor for heartfelt secrets
we separate inside dividing doors
coming to suspicion of each other
while longing for a sense of harmony
which is established with the grace of faith

who could prosper without a bracing faith?
who wants to wither behind boundaries
when we like the comfort of harmony
which is complicated by our secrets
as we are wary of one another
is it yet possible to open doors?

we get trapped within our protective doors
losing the innocence of childlike faith
because we are embittered with others
it's wise to make defensive boundaries
to be careful of a stranger's secrets
while fortifying inner harmony

we have need of natural harmony
every fortification needs a door
it's good to release each nagging secret
relying on an intuitive faith
making use of flexible boundaries
being skillful at addressing others

(. . . continued from page 81)

how can we learn to trust one another?
to enlarge our circle of harmony?
to live within communal boundaries?
to minimize sorting excluding doors?
to nurture tenuous and loving faith?
to overcome the poison of secrets?

we perpetuate sheltering secrets
we play civilizing games with others
depending on the fiber roots of faith
each of us grows with loving harmony
deploying tricks of diplomatic doors
preserving necessary boundaries

it's only human to have boundaries
we grow by fostering welcoming doors
we find our better selves in harmony.

From the car to the house I make one trip
I have a stubborn personality
the things I carry are easy to drop

two apples and a thermos of coffee
I can't really put them in my pockets
and I have two books additionally

this assorted caboodle doesn't fit
easily in my hands — I use my arms
to balance them — *I'm not using my wits* —

I make only one trip with no return
to the car — *so as not to waste my time* —
then there's the house key to clumsily turn

I stumble and bumble in the meantime
and muddle through — *I'll use a bag next time.*

A white murk encompasses Stillwater
the trees are encumbered within a mist
the outlines of the pines and leaves are blurred

on a chilly morning a fog persists
it appears our homes are inside a cloud
an eerie quiet other land exists

the spaciousness of distance is endowed
with a moist dripping air of mystery
the valley is hidden within a shroud

the sunrise is lost in uncertainty
yet a brightening tinge is a tip-off
it won't be long — *we will have clarity* —

the mystical ambience will burn off
this is a taste of a daybreak's send-off.

The rising sun doesn't dazzle my eyes
its facing fire doesn't glare anymore
summer's incandescence has passed on by

the earth and sun are playing tug-of-war
my eastward window is in sidelong shade
I know exactly what's happened before

within a month I will see a cascade
of oak leaves falling flowing from the west
as all the vibrancy of color fades

the trees are preparing to take a rest
they will be dormant throughout the winter
and yet the sun will continue to crest

the horizon — *earth's a twirling dancer*
sun embraces the role of romancer.

The misty sky is far above today
it appears as a vague grey/white ceiling
a cloud was amid our homes yesterday

these overcast skies can be appealing
they tower to indeterminate height
cumulative clouds are tranquilizing

in winter they are such a common sight
diminishing light merges together
day after day the difference is slight

one has to adapt to winter weather
I appreciate winter's subtle glow
winter's sunlight is soft as a feather

month after month the procession is slow
the circling of snow puts on a show.

I ate my last slice of watermelon
I'll have to wait for another summer
this is a loss that I will not dwell on

it's hardly a significant bummer
so many details are more important
I have blueberries and they taste better

certainly no reason to be mordant
I was getting bored of them anyway
are my missing melons *tragic? they ain't*

with no more troublesome rinds everyday
my garbage bags will be so much lighter
better without clutter to haul away

I enjoy life without watermelons
it's a lie that I am a hanger-on.

My key fob isn't working anymore
its battery reached the end of its zip
I need to be careful with my car doors

I'm going to have to use the metal tip
or to push the button inside the car
it is so easy to mentally slip

I've avoided embarrassment so far
and haven't locked myself out — *even once* —
It would be a predicament — by far

more cataclysmic — to be such a dunce
to be stranded on an icy evening
and so to experience every ounce

of shame — I don't want to be forgetting
what my absent-minded hands are doing.

Little annoyances will trip me up
follies happening absent-mindedly
encumbering me with silly screw-ups

I amble in my house confusedly
my feet wander — *my head is somewhere else* —
my thoughts are flying spontaneously

all while I securely fasten my belt
I'm not closing doors or shutting cupboards
once in a while I give myself a welt

I may not see what I am walking toward
the 100-pound dumbbell on the floor
not being mindful because I am bored

I've done it once — and many times before —

OW

can I not stub my big toe anymore?

What can be seen as unborn undying?
once the earth was nothing but swirling gas
the earth has a beginning and ending

we used to measure time with an hourglass
even the loftiest mountain breaks down
each in their turn the millennia pass

the sun with its weight swings the earth around
but can gravity be permanent when
the heat of the cosmos is winding down?

it's worth perplexity now and again
when cosmic theory becomes obsolete
to seek for faith as a safety pin

sky above our heads — ground beneath our feet
both are temporary — like a heartbeat.

Masquerade of Love Sestina

It doesn't do to be restless in love
to confuse love with possessive desire
to be sowing envious fearful seeds
that births a doubtful and anxious pattern
which prompts a self-punishing masquerade
dazed with the view of a funhouse mirror

seized by the sight of a funhouse mirror
one schemes and strives to be worthy of love
and then words and smiles are a masquerade
driven by lashes of ragged desire
when one gets trapped in a sleepless pattern
sowing precarious worrisome seeds

having sown a field of uncertain seeds
it's so easy to be frightened of mirrors
to assume a false and deceiving pattern
for the intoxicating lure of love
one may wake up in the grip of desire
startled by the pain of the masquerade

one resists the work of the masquerade
one reaps and hates the crop of bitter seeds
disliking the exhaustion of desire
when frustration is a hall of mirrors
with the stupidity that comes with love
in a narcotic and numbing pattern

(continued from page 91 . . .)

one begins to think of other patterns
that aren't dependent on a masquerade
there are hints of patience inside of love
there's an intuition for fruitful seeds
without compulsion for using mirrors
with a desire to escape desire

may we find our way to healthy desires
and discover liberating patterns
reflecting sunny cloud-dappled mirrors
where the trials of life are a masquerade
without effort sowing promising seeds
and not working so hard at knowing love

may we rest in the assurance of love
and reap the bounty of blossoming seeds
grateful for the tricks of the masquerade?

What is the nature of the masquerade?
who can be believed to be fooling whom?
who can be chided for being afraid?

as we're left on our own to face our doom
feeling vulnerable isolated
isn't it natural to issue gloom?

against circumstances I've debated
I have determined to seize what I need
my spirit and wits were armor-plated

to self-propulsion the direction leads
where winning was a duel of wits and will
only by victory could I be freed

I tended to make mountains from molehills
learning only lessons that fear instilled.

It's an intellectual paradox
there is every reason to be scheming
conniving to succeed is orthodox

it's honorable to be hard-working
to put our faith in careful industry
the American dream is inspiring

and depending on handouts is crazy
being motivated is paramount
there's no benefit from being lazy

there is pain in not getting what I want
I think my frustration is undeserved
and the success of others is a taunt

there is obsession about being served
with expectations over what's deserved.

Doing poetry is an act of love
part of me would like notoriety
would I enjoy being famous? — kind of

but I waffle in anonymity
a thimbleful of people know my name
as I scribble on in humility

celebrity's a fascinating game
I'm not sure that it ends with happiness
does celebrity overcome one's shame?

with poetry I experience bliss
juggling with words is clarifying
there's not a day writing I want to miss

the striving for fame is stupefying
crafting a poem is satisfying.

I waffle about in a masquerade
figuring out who I believe I am
I am sure it's not the Marquis de Sade

It's fallacious to propagate a scam
to think I'm a person who I am not
to be the one who is living a sham

there are battles I have already fought
it's no longer healthy to rage and blame
to have my stomach convulsing in knots

I recognize my nonsensical shame
I relax — and let it dissolve itself
the shame combusts in a propitious flame

It's good to be balanced within one's self
I've learned to be forgiving of myself.

It helps immensely to be with people
to share difficulties with each other
to get to know them if I am able

it is a truth that everyone suffers
I tend to believe that only I do
I wear my blinders and put up buffers

listening to people expands my view
there is so much that we share in common
we resemble chimpanzees in a zoo

our communal chatter we depend on
we gambol and shriek in the masquerade
it's our mutual grooming we count on

we chase each other in our chimp's charade
uttering noise in a crazy cascade.

Is a zoo a part of the masquerade?
are we being minded by a keeper?
every little transgression being weighted?

we are curious and we are seekers
it is so important to find what's true
we are sowers and then we are reapers

there are consequences for what we do
it is better not to worry so much
to assume that life's a dance of soft shoe

it doesn't help to demand overmuch
there are many ways to be ambitious
with my fellow chimps I like a soft touch

why waste energy being suspicious?
when an open heart is most propitious.

A wheelchair is a propitious way of
getting around for the disabled though
it comes with its drawbacks as I observed
River who is a beautiful cheerful
girl with a mop of curly brown hair *fall*
out of the chair when she was unbalanced
and the wheels rolled backwards and she called for
my help but I didn't understand what
she needed — *to stop the wheels rolling from*
behind — and so I watched her lurch from the
chair and *smack* on the floor *uttering pain*
and then she insisted on rising by
herself pulling her body into that
fickle chair again as I only watched.

She insists on doing
what she can denying
multiple sclerosis
its victory *as most*
of us are ignorant.

ah

—Tekkan

www.ingramcontent.com/pod-product-compliance
Lightning Source LLC
LaVergne TN
LVHW010356160826
845677LV00005BA/1293
* 9 7 9 8 9 8 6 7 2 6 2 1 2 *